COME, FOLLOW ME

On the Life of Discipleship

H.H. POPE SHENOUDA III

Translated by
St. Mary and St. Moses Abbey

ST
Mary
&
Moses
ABBEY PRESS

Come, Follow Me: On the Life of Discipleship
By Pope Shenouda III

Translated from Arabic by St. Mary & St. Moses Abbey.

Copyright © 2024 Coptic Orthodox Diocese of the Southern U.S.A.

Designed & Published by:
St. Mary & St. Moses Abbey Press
101 S Vista Dr., Sandia, TX 78383
stmabbeypress.com

Contents

The Life of Discipleship

Christian life is a life of discipleship.

All those who believed in Christ were called His disciples. He, however, was called "Teacher" and "good Teacher." And although all were discipled unto him, He had private disciples who were called "His own."[1] These He prepared for the ministry of the word[2], and concerning these it was said that "when He had called His twelve disciples to Him, He gave them power over unclean spirits, to cast them out."[3]

It was said in the Sermon on the Mount, "His disciples came to Him. Then He opened His mouth and taught them."[4] And when He wanted to celebrate the Passover, He sent two of His disciples to say that "the Teacher says, 'Where is the guest room in

---

1   John 13:1.

2   See Acts 6:4.

3   Matthew 10:1.

4   Matthew 5:1–2.

which I may eat the Passover with My disciples?'"[5]

Likewise the followers of John the Baptist were called his disciples. It was said that once "there arose a dispute between some of John's disciples and the Jews about purification."[6] And on another occasion, the disciples of John came to the Lord Christ, saying, "Why do we and the Pharisees fast often, but Your disciples do not fast?"[7]

The Pharisees also used to call themselves the disciples of Moses. Therefore, in the argument between the Jews and the man who was born blind whom the Lord granted sight, they said to him, "You are His disciple, but we are Moses' disciples."[8]

We also note that preaching was called discipleship. For when the Lord sent His disciples to preach the gospel, He said to them, "Go therefore and make disciples of all the nations, baptizing them … teaching them to observe all things that I have commanded you."[9] And when Paul and Barnabas went to Derbe, it was said that "they had preached the gospel to that city and made many disciples."[10]

---

5   Mark 14:14.
6   John 3:25.
7   Matthew 9:14.
8   John 9:28.
9   Matthew 28:19–20.
10   Acts 14:21.

The Conditions of Discipleship

On the subject of discipleship, we would like to make two remarks:

1. Discipleship is not unto the teaching only, but unto the life also.

2. Therefore, discipleship has conditions that must be fulfilled in the practical life.

And thus the Lord says to His disciples, "If you abide in My word, you are My disciples indeed."[11] Only hearing the words from the teacher does not then mean that a person is discipled unto him, but abiding in his teaching. The meaning of this is the transformation of words to life and to rooted principles which abide in the one who is taught.

The Lord Christ gives us a sign and a practical example, by saying to His disciples, "By this all will know that you are My disciples, if you have love for one another."[12] Here He presents a condition,

---

11   John 8:31.
12   John 13:35.

without which they are not His disciples, no matter how much theoretical knowledge they receive from Him concerning love. And if people do not find this mutual love in them, they cannot say that these are the disciples of Christ. It is a required sign. As Christ loved all, so His disciples must [love all] too. "As He walked,"[13] they also ought to walk.

This reminds me of the saying of the Lord to the Jews who boasted of being Abraham's children, "If you were Abraham's children, you would do the works of Abraham."[14]

True discipleship is then a discipleship unto a life, which is made manifest practically in man's life, through which he declares that he is discipled unto a teacher distinguished for this kind of life and for this style[15] of teaching.

And for this reason, the Lord Christ presents specimens of people who cannot be His disciples, of which are the following. "If anyone comes to Me and does not hate his father and mother, wife and children, brothers and sisters, yes, and his own life also, he cannot be My disciple. And whoever does not bear his cross and come after Me cannot be My disciple.... So likewise, whoever of you does not forsake all that he has cannot be My disciple."[16]

---

13   1 John 2:6.

14   John 8:39.

15   Literally: color.

16   Luke 14:26–27, 33.

And so, the Lord Christ put in place rules[17] for discipleship unto Him, which are, renunciation and the love of God above the love of relatives. From this standpoint, His disciple Peter said to Him, "See, we have left all and followed You."[18] So the Lord answered him, with the same spiritual teaching, "Everyone who has left houses or brothers or sisters or father or mother or wife or children or lands, for My name's sake, shall receive a hundredfold, and inherit eternal life."[19]

Thus it is a principle in the discipleship unto the Lord, that you abandon everything for His sake—or that you, in your heart at least, are ready to abandon everything—and you do not regret doing so.

And for this reason, the Lord added another condition, which is, "No one, having put his hand to the plow, and looking back, is fit for the kingdom of God."[20] For discipleship unto the Lord requires steadfastness in the path and not going back. It also requires that a man endures for the sake of the Lord and His service, and that he labors for its sake. Therefore, the Lord said, "And whoever does not bear his cross and come after Me cannot be My disciple."[21]

17　Literally: a rule.
18　Matthew 19:27.
19　Matthew 19:29.
20　Luke 9:62.
21　Luke 14:27.

There are other conditions for discipleship, such as implementation and commitment. For the person who would like to be discipled unto Him must be committed to what he hears and must implement it, and so he transforms knowledge to life. For what profit do words [alone] have, if we were to hear them and [then] forget them, or to keep them in our minds for the sake of mere knowledge only?

Therefore, how beautiful is that phrase which those visiting the fathers said, "Give me a word, by which I may live." For the word is their spiritual food; they take it and nourish their spirit with it, so they live by it and benefit—not only intellectual benefit, but they benefit by it in their practical life, so it [that is, a word] becomes a word of benefit.

Word of Benefit

The spiritual person is discipled unto the word of benefit. They search for it from all sources:[22] from the Holy Scriptures first, from the sayings of the fathers, from trust-worthy teachers, and from any [other] source, and even if a word is from a sinful mouth, it is nevertheless beneficial.

Of such is the story of St. Ephraim and the woman who gazed at him:

> A female of careless life … fixed her eyes intently upon him; he rebuked her, and commanded her to look down upon the ground, "Wherefore should I obey your injunction," replied the woman; "for I was born not of the earth, but of you? It would be more just if you were to look down upon the earth whence you sprang, while I look upon you, as I was born of you."[23]

22   Literally: all its sources.

23   Sozomen *The Ecclesiastical History of Sozomen* III.XVI (NPNF[2] 2).

So the saint benefited from the woman's word and trained himself to look down to the earth. Likewise St. Anthony benefited from the word of the woman who took her clothes off and went down to bathe in front of him:

> The saint said to her, "Woman, are you not ashamed to take your clothes off in front of me, and I am a monk?" The woman answered him, "If you had been a monk, you would have dwelled in the inner desert, for this place is not fitting for monks to dwell in." So St. Anthony benefited exceedingly from her word, and said to himself, "This is the voice of God through the mouth of this woman." And he arose and went into the desert.[24]

In the past, people were accustomed to traversing land and sea, in long journeys, to ask one of the fathers for a word of benefit. *The Paradise of the Fathers* is full of stories of this kind. The travels of Palladius, Jerome, and Rufinus are all of this kind, and their books have left us invaluable heritage which have benefited the world spiritually.

And the matter was not limited to the young and commoner, but even those who held great positions also sought a word of benefit. For example, Pope

---

24   Cf. *Bostan Al-Rohban Al-Mowasah, Al-joz' Al-Awal* [The Expanded Paradise of the Monks, Volume 1]. (Egypt: St. Macarius Monastery, 2006), 33.

Theophilus, the 23rd Patriarch, many a time came to monasteries to be given a word of benefit from the holy monks. And his stories are well-known when he visited Abba Arsenius[25] and Abba Paphnutius[26]. Likewise is the visit of Pope Benjamin, the 38th Patriarch, to the monasteries and dwellings of the solitaries. It is also well-known that Pope Athanasius the Apostolic was discipled unto Abba Anthony the Great.

We hear of Abba Macarius the Great, that he asked for a word of benefit from the boy Zechariah:

> Abba Macarius said unto Abba Zechariah, "Tell me, what is the work of monks?" He said unto him, "Do you ask me, father?" The old man said unto me, "I beseech you, my son, Zechariah, for there is something which is right I should ask you." And Abba Zechariah said unto him, "Father, I give it as my opinion that the work of monks consists in a man restraining himself in everything."[27]

---

25 See *The Paradise of the Holy Fathers* 2, A.W. Budge, trans. (London, UK: Chatto & Windus, 1907), 14.

26 See *Bostan Al-Rohban Al-Mowasah, Al-joz' Al-Awal* [The Expanded Paradise of the Monks, Part 1]. (Egypt: St. Macarius Monastery, 2006), 421.

27 *The Paradise of the Holy Fathers* 2, A.W. Budge, trans. (London, UK: Chatto & Windus, 1907), 174. The version of the story mentioned in the Arabic text goes as follows: "Therefore the boy marveled and said to him, 'You, my father, are the star of the desert and its lighthouse, and are you asking for a word from me who is little?' So St. Macarius answered him humbly, 'I trust, my son, in the Holy Spirit who is in you,

We also hear of Abba Macarius, that he took a word of benefit from a boy who was herding cows.[28]

Discipleship is not impeded by age or position, and blessed is the person who lives as a disciple their whole life.

Our problem is that we think that we know or that we have reached the point in which we do not need to ask or to learn; while we find a group like the Apostles of the Lord Christ, asking Him once, saying, "Lord, teach us to pray."[29] Who of people did not know how to pray? Everyone knows— or they think they know. But the Apostles asked something that appears evident! And the result was that the Lord taught them the Lord's prayer, and it was beneficial.

From here, one of the attributes of discipleship is humility. It begins by a person feeling that he needs to learn, and to ask, and to seek counsel; and by his feeling that other [people] understand more than him, and that God is able to give to other [people] that with which they may guide him.

Concerning the humility of discipleship, see what St. Paul the Apostle said about himself, that he was brought up and disciplined "at the feet of

---

that you have something the knowledge of which I lack.'"

28 See *The Anonymous Sayings of the Desert Fathers*, J. Wortley, trans. (Cambridge, UK: Cambridge University Press, 2013), N490bis.

29 Luke 11:1.

Gamaliel,"[30] in that the disciple could not sit on the same level with his teacher, but rather sits at his feet.

And of the conditions of discipleship also is that the things you hear, you should keep well within you, so that you do not forget them. As David the prophet said, "Your word I have hidden in my heart, that I might not sin against You."[31]

Forgetting a commandment makes you fall into sin and makes you forget the principles and values you want to be discipled unto; therefore, the Lord said:

> And these words which I command you today shall be in your heart. You shall teach them diligently to your children, and shall talk of them when you sit in your house, when you walk by the way, when you lie down, and when you rise up. You shall bind them as a sign on your hand, and they shall be as frontlets between your eyes. You shall write them on the doorposts of your house and on your gates.[32]

All this is so that you do not forget it. You should also do likewise, so that you do not forget your spiritual practices.

---

30 Acts 22:3.

31 Psalms 119:11.

32 Deuteronomy 6:6–9.

For you are discipled, through receiving knowledge; you then move to the stage of application through practices. You ought to always place your practices in front of your eyes, so they may be in your memory, to warn you whenever you are fought with breaking them.

Discipleship unto a Life

Not only are you discipled unto the teachers' words, but also unto their life, even without their speaking. You soak up [the manner of] life from them, the good example and laudable model which they possess.

Therefore, the ear is not the only means for learning, but the eye also. It is related concerning Abba Sisoes, that, out of his profound humility, he did not give a teaching to his disciple. So when the fathers reproached him for having given no guidance to the new brother, to whom they had entrusted him to teach, he said to them, "I am not an abbot nor a teacher. If he wants to learn something, let him see how I act and work, and let him do like me, without me giving him an order."[33]

And of the examples of learning from the manner of life is the following. [It happened that] three brethren visited Abba Anthony. Two of them asked

---

33 Cf. *The Paradise of the Holy Fathers* 2, A.W. Budge, trans. (London, UK: Chatto & Windus, 1907), 103–104.

him [questions], but the third sat in silence. When the saint inquired, as to why he asked nothing, the brother answered him, saying, "It is enough for me to see your face, father."[34]

Only seeing the face of the saint was a lesson from which the brother learned, in silence. He sees how the saint speaks and gives answers, and looks at his meek, calm, humble countenance—and he learns.

[Here is] another example. Pope Theophilus once visited Scetis. The fathers said to Abba Paphnutius, "Say a word, that the Pope may be benefited." He answered them, "If he has not benefited from my silence, neither will he benefit from my words."[35]

Truly silence can be discipled unto, exactly as words of benefit.

And perhaps one of the most beautiful examples of this is Abba Arsenius the Great, unto whose silence many were discipled, benefiting of his good example more than the words of other teachers.

And likewise now one may be discipled unto others' lives, unto their beautiful attributes, and may soak up their virtues, without their giving him lessons on these virtues. And so did St. Anthony do, in the first stage of his monastic life, for he was

---

34   Cf. *Give Me a Word: The Alphabetical Sayings of the Desert Fathers*, Wortley J., trans. (Yonkers, NY: SVS Press, 2014), Anthony 27.
35   Cf. *Give Me a Word: The Alphabetical Sayings of the Desert Fathers*, Wortley J., trans. (Yonkers, NY: SVS Press, 2014), Theophilus 2.

accustomed to learning from the life of the ascetics he saw.[36] He was like a bee extracting nectar from every flower, learning from one ascetic stillness, humility from another, silence from a third [ascetic], speaking well from a fourth.

What St. Anthony did reminds us of another beneficial teaching: Do not try, in your [life of] discipleship, to be a carbon copy of a single person particularly. For there is no single person among the sons of men who has all the virtues. Also what is suitable for a particular person might not be suitable for you yourself. Take, rather, from every person what you admire of their beautiful qualities. And of these qualities take the measure which is good for you, and in the manner that fits your disposition, mentality, and circumstances.

And so discipleship is unto the life [of another], and from this [comes] the discipleship unto the biographies of the saints. And on this St. Paul the Apostle says, "Remember those who rule over you, who have spoken the word of God to you, whose faith follow, considering the outcome of their conduct."[37]

The Holy Scriptures have presented to us practical examples of every kind. Also history has

---

36   See Athanasius *Life of Antony* 3–4. *In Nicene and Post-Nicene Fathers: Second Series* 4, P. Schaff, ed. (Peabody, MA: Hendrickson Publishers, 2012), 196.
37   Hebrews 13:7.

presented to us other examples in all the branches of virtue and in all the walks of life, which we may be discipled unto.

The Lord Christ reproved the Jews with the example of the queen of the South, saying to them, "The queen of the South will rise up in the judgment with this generation and condemn it, for she came from the ends of the earth to hear the wisdom of Solomon; and indeed a greater than Solomon is here."[38] She was a marvelous example of seeking wisdom and knowledge, that is, discipleship. She was discipled unto a man who took wisdom from God Himself, and who was wiser than all the people of his generation.[39] This queen became an example for us to imitate.

The Lord presented examples to His generation and to us, unto whom we may be discipled.

He presented to us the Canaanite woman in her humility. She said about herself and her daughter, "Yet even the little dogs eat the crumbs which fall from their masters' table."[40]

The Lord also presented to us the example of the centurion in his faith, who said, "Lord, I am not worthy that You should come under my roof. But only speak a word, and my servant will be

---

38   Matthew 12:42.

39   See 1 Kings 3:12.

40   Matthew 15:27.

healed."[41] So the Lord said to those who followed Him, "Assuredly, I say to you, I have not found such great faith, not even in Israel!"[42]

And so the Lord presented living examples to the people, of those living around them, who are suitable as a model to be discipled unto their example.

He also presented to them the example of the widow who gave out of her poverty[43], and the example of the woman who poured the very costly oil of spikenard on His head at the house of Simon the leper, and He said, "Assuredly, I say to you, wherever this gospel is preached in the whole world, what this woman has done will also be told as a memorial to her."[44]

Thus, the examples, whom you are discipled unto, are not only the saints who have departed, but also the living examples around you.

And you perhaps find in these whom you associate and mingle with, and in those who live in your generation though you do not mingle with them—you perhaps find in these and those good examples you are able to pick up, soak up, and imitate.

We see in children an example of those who learn

---

41   Matthew 8:8.
42   Matthew 8:10.
43   See Mark 12:44.
44   Mark 14:9.

through emulation. They have not yet reached the degree of intellectual understanding and maturity that would help them in receiving knowledge or understanding advice. They, however, live like those around them live. They take life, religion, and everything by way of handing down, rather than by way of learning.

And as you learn from the virtues of people, so can you learn from their mistakes. For, seeing the mistake and its bad consequences and others' reactions to it, you can take a lesson on avoiding this mistake in your life. Or as the lion said, "Fox, who taught you wisdom?" He answered, "I learned it from the wolf's head flying off his corpse."

And how beautiful is the proverb that says: "I have learned silence from the parrot." That is to say, when I saw the evils of much talking, I took a lesson on the sublimity of silence and its benefit, and on respecting those who maintain silence.

Lessons from Death

You learn from life, and you also learn from death. It is a great teacher to you and to others.

Many of the fathers took from death a lesson on renunciation and a lesson that the world is passing away, and its lusts will be abolished. And the profundity of this feeling led some of them into monasticism and the abandonment of the world in its entirety.

An example of such is the great saint Abba Anthony. He beheld his father on his death bed, motionless, so he spoke to him, saying, "Where are your power, your greatness, and your wealth? You have gone out of the world against your will. But I will go out by my will, before they cast me out [of it] reluctantly." And so he determined on monasticism. And having this feeling in his heart, he was influenced by a verse he heard in the church (Matthew 19:21).[45]

45   See *Bostan Al-Rohban Al-Mowasah, Al-joz' Al-Awal* [The Expanded Paradise of the Monks, Part 1]. (Egypt: St. Macarius Monastery, 2006),

The saint Abba Paul the first hermit was influenced by death too. He was on his way to court, to settle a dispute with his relative over inheritance. On the way, he saw a funeral procession. Influenced, he left the money and the dispute, and went into the desert in pursuit of the salvation of his soul.[46]

There is a story also of Abba Macarius giving advice to a brother:

> Abba Macarius said unto him, "Go to the cemetery and revile the dead;" and he went and reviled them and stoned them with stones.... And the old man said unto him, "Do they say nothing unto you?" and the brother said unto him, "No." And again the old man said unto him, "Go tomorrow and praise them, and call them, 'Apostles, saints, and righteous men.'" And he came to the old man, and said, "I have praised them." And the old man said unto him, "And did they return no answer to you?" and he said, "No." And the old man said unto him, "…. And thus let it be with yourself. If you wish to live[47], become dead, so that you may care neither for the reviling of men nor for their praise, for the dead care for nothing."[48]

33–34.

46 Ibid., 27.

47 Arabic text has "to be a monk" instead of "to live."

48 *The Paradise of the Holy Fathers* 2, A.W. Budge, trans. (London, UK: Chatto & Windus, 1907), 104–105.

Once Abba Macarius, going to sleep, placed a skull under his head.[49] Some of the saints would spiritually benefit from the sight of skulls, from seeing a dead person, and from visiting cemeteries, but [even] the mere mention of death would benefit them, and the meditation on it was a spiritual lesson for them.

It was said concerning Alexander the Great, the greatest leader and emperor in his generation, that he charged one of his servants to say to him daily, "Remember that you are a man, and will inevitably die one day."

I wish that you would benefit from every death you hear of and from every funeral you attend, and would be discipled unto those whom death influenced, who took profitable lessons from it.

---

49   See ibid., 197.

Discipleship unto Books

Discipleship is originally unto fathers and teachers. And as the poet said, "Take knowledge from its masters, and seek wisdom from the wise."

What happens if you do not find a teacher, a father, nor a guide; there are then books, which contain everything. They may profit you even in the presence of a guide too.

Origen, the greatest scholar in his time, was discipled unto books. It was said of him that he used to rent libraries and stay overnight in them, continuing to read throughout the night, devouring the treasures of knowledge that are in the manuscripts. About him St. Jerome said, "He would read while eating, read while walking ... until his mind was filled with knowledge." Origen, however, suffered harm from some of his readings.

And in our present time, we make mention of Habib Guirguis, who, having found no teacher in the theological college from whom he may receive knowledge—especially after the repose of Hegumen Philotheos Ibrahim—resorted to books, voraciously devouring the knowledge they contained. And he became the greatest[50] teacher of theology in his generation, and he wrote on doctrine, on spirituality, on the histories of the saints, and on curricula for church education and religious teaching. The source of his knowledge was books.

The person, however, must carefully choose the books they read and will be discipled unto, and must read with discernment and care, and must not adopt everything they read. For there are books, even by renowned authors, that contain unsound information. And not all books are without error. Therefore, the reader should place in front of themself the saying of St. Paul the Apostle, "Test all things; hold fast what is good. Abstain from every form of evil;"[51] and the saying of St. John also, "Do not believe every spirit, but test the spirits, whether they are of God."[52]

The person must also distinguish between reading and application. There are spiritual principles that require guidance in their application, and some virtues might require that they be practiced extremely gradually. Someone might read in *the Paradise of the Fathers* about a virtue which was acquired by one of

---

50   Literally: first.

51   1 Thessalonians 5:21.

52   1 John 4:1.

the saints—and perhaps the saint reached this after years of struggle—does the reader then take this as a starting point, imitating what the saint reached at the end, without emulating the saint's gradual approach and struggle?

We say this concerning some of the degrees of prayer, silence, fasting, solitude, and the like matters whose practice requires spiritual guidance.

Thanks be to God that the Coptic library currently treasures many valuable books, whether translated books of the saying of the fathers, or the lives of the saints, or spiritual, doctrinal, historical, ritual books, and all various forms of knowledge.

The person must choose what satisfies their heart and mind, and must create for themselves a daily program for reading, or at least a weekly program, so that if the person falls short one day, the reading of the following day will sustain them.

Servants especially need more reading, that they may satisfy their disciples. And this is so that they do not present to them repetitive or superficial information they already know. Undoubtedly, the servant who has profound knowledge, the disciples sense the richness of his information; therefore, they flock to him and his lessons. And the servant cannot make them disciples, unless he himself was made a disciple first, and has dived deeper in his knowledge. As the maxim says, "Be filled up, for nothing overflows except that which was filled up."

Discipleship unto books has two aspects: knowledge and life.

To turn some of what you know into life, you should take on spiritual exercises. Read and understand well. Extract the spiritual, profitable meanings, which are suitable for you, and keep a record of them in your personal notebook, so that you may be reminded of them from time to time. Train yourself unto them and hold yourself accountable for the exercise. Keep watch over yourself regarding the application and reproach yourself if you fall short. And so you turn the spiritual information into life.

In speaking about books and Origen, we mention two [men], St. Basil the Great and St. Gregory the Theologian, who were discipled unto him, though they were not his contemporaries but lived in the century following his. Nevertheless, they were discipled unto his books, exactly like what the Jews said to the man born blind, "We are Moses' disciples."[53] Though they were not contemporaries of Moses the prophet, but they were discipled unto the five books he wrote, which were called the Law of Moses, [Pentateuch].

You have undoubtedly met many good people. So have you benefited from them? Believe me that God will condemn us on the Last Day, if we do not benefit from the excellent characters whom He sent

---

53 John 9:28.

to us to imitate. It is as He said to the contemporaries of His life in the flesh on earth, "The queen of the South will rise up in the judgment with this generation and condemn it."[54]

Perhaps you hear or read about meekness, but you do not exactly understand its meaning. Then God sends you a meek person whom you see and so you are discipled unto his meekness. And you understand from him what meekness is, more than what books have explained.

And so of every virtue, the Lord sends us living specimens: of humility, simplicity, godly zeal, faith, all manner of spiritual matters which books are incapable of explaining with precision, and whose meaning may be more than what the expression of terms can harbor. And if God asks, "Why were you not discipled unto these practical models?" Then "every mouth may be stopped."[55]

Do you think that discipleship is only unto books, sermons, and spiritual guidance? No, for there are people who do not speak about virtues; rather their virtues speak about them.

Therefore, take a lesson from every virtue you see in any person, whoever they may be, Christian or non-Christian, a clergyman or layman.

---

54   Matthew 12:42.

55   Romans 3:19.

Discipleship unto Nature

When I speak about nature, I would like to mention the saying of the psalm: "The heavens declare the glory of God; and the firmament shows His handiwork."[56] Yes, nature speaks; therefore, the psalmist continues in this psalm, saying, "Day unto day utters speech, and night unto night reveals knowledge."[57]

It is possible then for a person to hear the speeches of nature, the speech of the heavens and the firmament. So what are the lessons which we learn when we are discipled unto nature. I would like to mention the following lessons from nature.

1. A Lesson on Order and Precision. Foremost on this is the marvelous and precise order binding the sun, moon, and the stars. How the earth turns around its axis in an ordered fashion every twenty-four hours, resulting in the night and day [cycles]. And it also circles around the sun every year,

56   Psalms 19:1.
57   Psalms 19:2.

resulting in the four seasons. All this [has continued] with such an order that has not gone amiss at all throughout thousands of years, to the extent that a person can predict what will happen in the coming hours, days, or months, with respect to the pressure of the air, the wind, rain, cold, and the sea. Also the succession of seasons and times according to the precise order of nature, is a lesson for us.

The systems of the human body are an example of [nature's] order and precision. We mean these systems as God created them, and not as are corrupted by a person through negligence or by suffering from an illness, infection, and accidents. These are very precise systems and well-ordered, whether in the function of the heart and the circulation of blood in the human body, or the function of the brain with all its centers, or the digestive system, or the nervous system, or others. Contemplate the eye as a meticulous system, or the ear as a system for hearing, or the tongue as a system for tasting and speaking and for helping the digestive system. [This is] truly marvelous, to the extent that they used to study medicine in theological schools, because it gives an idea about God's power in creation.

2. A Lesson on Working Tirelessly, Without Asking for Taking a Rest. Imagine if the earth leaned back onto its axis, asking for a little rest from the toil of this endless spinning, what disturbance would then ensue in the light and darkness? The earth, however, never stops working, and neither do the moon and the rest of the members of the solar system, of sun, planets, and stars. It is an unceasing work and a marvelous activity, for the sake of accomplishing their mission with all faithfulness. All these are lessons for us.

3. A Lesson on Working for the Sake of Others, Carrying out Another's Will, With All Obedience and All Faithfulness. Truly, what profit does nature itself obtain from all the work it does? What does water benefit from evaporating by heat, rising up, then becoming condensed as rain, and falling down to the earth? And it continues to rise up and fall down every season, every year, for the sake of another.

Nature, in its entirety, works in the service of others. Its own self, however, has no place in its work. It gives and that is it. It obeys the law God placed for it and does not deviate from or discuss it. Indeed, what would have happened, had the planets held a council, to discuss their plan for work for the coming year? Or, if they asked to manage their own affairs? Or, if they protested against the continual work—nonstop and with no vacation?

The one who does these is the rational man, whose mind troubles him, who does not learn a lesson from nature, nor does he perform what he says to God, "Your will be done on earth as it is in heaven."[58]

---

58   Matthew 6:10.

4. A Lesson on Cooperation and Teamwork. The entirety of nature works together, to accomplish one duty. It suffices that a person eats a meal, to find that the hands work in presenting the food, the teeth breaking it up, the tongue turning it around and hurling it to the pharynx, esophagus, and the stomach; [and you find that there are] secretions from here and there, that what is beneficial may be absorbed and turned into blood, tissues, and energy, while the excess the intestine eliminates to the outside. Every organ and system in the body works with the rest of the organs, for the sake of the good of the whole body, in a marvelous cooperation, receiving [something] from an organ to pass it to another, partnering with another. [This is] to the extent that we cannot ultimately say who did the work; for it was the entire digestive system [working together]. But even the rest of the systems were working with it, like the heart, brain, etc., though the work was attributed to the digestive system alone.

The same cooperation we see among the temperature, wind, rain, and plants. All work together, for the sake of sound performance, to profit the whole. A part of nature cannot, on its own, do a work alone. And the same cooperation we find in the kingdom of the ants and bees, in a marvelous partnership which time fails me to speak of.

Can we not learn this lesson from nature?

5. A Lesson Which the Holy Scripture Spoke of: "If one member suffers, all the members suffer with it."[59] It suffices that one member suffers, to find the nervous system intervening, the feeling of pain becoming manifest, and perhaps sirens sounding, to prompt its treatment: a siren from the temperature of the body, a siren from the heartbeats, from blood pressure, from a headache, or others. All of these cry out, saying, "There is a sickness here, treat it." If a microbe enters the body, you find a tireless movement by the white blood cells, and you find all the resistance systems get ready to fight, beside the aid from the limbs and the brain, etc.

The Apostle continues his word and says, "Or if one member is honored, all the members rejoice with it."[60] The countenance smiles, the heart is assured, the nerves calm down, and the hands and feet arise to serve and express their joy. It is a lesson nature presents on the feelings of the one family.

6. A Lesson on Working Without Being Affected by People's Opinion of it. Rain falls in its appointed time and does its duty, without being affected by the thanksgiving of the farmer whose crop it waters; nor is it affected by the grumbling of the person who was drenched by it, or the hut which fell down from the downpour, or the clothes that were soaked. Rain does not seek vainglory; therefore,

---

59   1 Corinthians 12:26.

60   Ibid.

it is not affected by praise or disparagement. For it, it suffices that it does its duty faithfully.

Likewise are the sun, heat, cold, and wind, too. They do their duty and do not care about the praise of the one who is pleased, nor the objection of the one who is annoyed. Rather, performing the duty is their sole occupation.

7. A Lesson on Wisdom. Contemplate the vineyard, for example. It shakes down its leaves in winter, to give you an opportunity to enjoy the rays of the sun under the trellis it climbs onto. Then it returns to be clothed with leaves in summer, for then you need the shade and not the warmth. And in like manner, we can speak of the royal poinciana tree, a shade tree, and many of the trees that shake down their leaves.

Of the wisdom also is that many plants and fruits become available at a good time, suitable for man. Watermelon, for example, becomes available in summer, for you need to quench your thirst with its water, because of the heat, while oranges become available in winter, for you need the vitamin C they contain, to guard yourself against catching a cold. In the same manner, many of the fruits may be taken as a source for meditation on the wisdom of the time of their appearing.

8. A Lesson on Self-denial. We take this lesson from roots, for example. They remain concealed in the ground, not being manifest, while they bear the whole tree. As a tree grows up in height, so the roots grow more branched, becoming more hidden in the earth, that by going down, they give the tree an opportunity to go up. Is this called sacrifice or love, humility or self-denial, or serving others, or all these together? And it is so.

Imagine if the roots suffered from jealousy, envying the trunk, stem, branches, and leaves, for being manifest and for people's praise of them, and so they desired to be like them!—therefore, the root abandoned its earth and hiddenness, and rose up like the leaves dancing in the air—would not the whole tree collapse? But we thank God, that the roots do not act so. They are humble, steadfast in their humility, and are not prone to jealousy.

The same lesson we take from foundations of buildings. People praise the skyscraper for its architecture, spaciousness, height, decorations, lighting, furniture, etc. As for the foundation, hidden under the earth, no one speaks of it, while it is the one bearing the entire building. But it possesses self-denial. As the building goes up, so the foundation goes down. It does not look for praise, but for the safety of the visible [part of the] building. As for the foundation, being in the depth is sufficient for it.

9. A Lesson on the Diversity of the Virtues. As we saw, the matter is not restricted to a single virtue, but is a bouquet of various colors. For while the flower gives you an idea on beauty and giving, the fruit gives you an idea on living to give itself for the life of another; yet another fruit is for treatment. And there is a fruit that accepts to be bitter in taste, for so it is good for health.

10. A Lesson on Power and Resilience. A mountain or a hill is an example of that. No matter how fiercely the wind blows and how much rain falls upon it, it remains firm, immovable. And no matter how many caves or roads man bores into it, and no matter the number of buildings established upon it, it remains standing, unshaken. Rocks in rapids are another example. Although water and waves crash into them, they are firm, not bothered by the collision, and are not affected by them.

11. A Lesson on Adapting to the Environment. Desert plants, which do not find water for themselves, do not present their leaves for evaporation and transpiration. Rather they are folded in a needle-like manner, so as not to lose water. The arctic bear and fox are another example, which have fur protecting them against the cold, while the skin of a horse is the opposite of that, because the horse does not live in a cold environment. Do we take from this another lesson in God's care for His creatures? Yes, we undoubtedly do.

12. All Things Work Together for Good, which is a Lesson in Faith. Thorns in the previous point remind us that all things work together for good.

A literary writer said a wise word: "Even thorns can work as fertilizer for the field." And there is nothing strange in that, because thorns, if burned, turn into ashes, and ashes work as fertilizer, thereby benefiting the person. This is beside another benefit resulting from burning them, that is, warmth, or the employment of the heat for other benefits. This gives us another lesson, in that we should benefit from everything, even the thorns which may appear harmful at first glance.

13. A Lesson on Humility. This lesson we take from the clouds and water. Water evaporates, thereby becoming lighter, and rises up and becomes clouds. It does not, however, forget its origin, that it was at underground level. And so it becomes humble, because it knows that this height will not last. The time will come, in which it will be cooled and condense, and the wind will blow, making it fall to the ground. The roots of a tree might absorb it, thereby it descends below the ground.

Can the clouds, I wonder, boast against the water, when they know their origin and fate? Or is it possible that [a drop of] water suffers from low self-esteem upon the mention of its colleagues of drops which have evaporated and risen up? No, for both are satisfied with their state, whether God lifted it up to heaven [or sky] or brought it down to the earth, or whether the tree roots absorbed it, or whether it entered into the veins of leaves or branches. This is another lesson on the life of submission.

14. A Lesson from Manure. We may take a lesson from the manure used to fertilize the ground. A person may see it and hold it in contempt, because of its stench and its bad looks. Nevertheless, the manure is satisfied with the state it is in, and God who created it is able to change it. For it may become part of the food of a tree, which absorbs it and carries it as nourishment for its buds; therefore, it turns into a fruit which a person eats, and thereby it enters into the composition of a person's body. And it may turn into a tissue in a person.

Does a person, I wonder, become humble, when they realize that some of their tissues were one day manure in the earth? All these are spiritual lessons for whoever desires to learn and meditate, which remind us of the Lord's saying, "Take heed that you do not despise one of these little ones."[61]

15. A Lesson that God Takes Care of us and Cares About us. This is made clear from the saying of the Lord:

> Consider the lilies of the field, how they grow: they neither toil nor spin; and yet I say to you that even Solomon in all his glory was not arrayed like one of these. Now if God so clothes the grass of the field, which today is, and tomorrow is thrown into the oven, will He not much more clothe you, O

---

61   Matthew 18:10.

you of little faith?[62]

It is a lesson on not worrying about our needs, for God is the One who takes care of us, without our asking.

Truly God, when He put Adam in Paradise, put him in a place full of spiritual benefits, to the one who contemplates. God gave him the right to have dominion over the earth and subdue it.[63] But it was more beneficial for him to contemplate and learn, [and] not have dominion!

---

62 Matthew 6:28–30.
63 See Genesis 1:26, 28.

Discipleship unto the Animal Kingdom

This is another point on the sources of discipleship. This principle the Lord presented to us when He said, "Be wise as serpents and harmless as doves."[64] He gave us a lesson that we should learn simplicity[65] from doves and wisdom from serpents. This is a symbol or inspiration that we learn even from the birds and the creeping things of the earth.

Lessons from a Sparrow

Believe me [when I say] that I have learned many lessons from a sparrow. I was [once] sitting in front of my cell in the garden of the monastery, and there were some seeds on the ground, which may have fallen from one of the farm workers. A sparrow flew

---

64   Matthew 10:16.

65   "Simplicity" is a derivative of the word used in the Arabic verse. The word appears as "harmless" in NKJV.

in to peck at the seed. I supposed that it would eat to its fill from these provisions, but it pecked at a seed or two and flew away, leaving all this goodness behind it, without caring about it nor being sorry for it.

I learned from it a lesson on contentment, but also on renunciation. I was reminded by the Lord's saying that "they neither sow nor reap nor gather into barns."[66] This sparrow did not linger around this material good, nor did it make for itself a permanent abode beside it. It rather took the bare minimum it wanted and flew away, more joyful to soar in the air than to sit beside the material on the earth. This was a profitable lesson for me.

It was singing joyfully, having abandoned everything. And I said to myself, "This sparrow is more of a monk than me." For it did all this by its nature and disposition, without exerting any effort, without resisting an inner feeling. Joy is of its nature, despite that there might be small snares awaiting it. And I remembered the saying of the Apostle, "Rejoice in the Lord always."[67]

The sparrow gave me a lesson on the life of faith. For it left the quantity of seeds and flew away, trusting fully that wherever it goes, it will find its sustenance and food, caring about nothing. And here I remembered the Lord's saying, "Do not worry

66   Matthew 6:26.
67   Philippians 4:4.

about tomorrow, for tomorrow will worry about its own things,"[68] and, "Do not worry about your life, what you will eat or what you will drink,"[69] and His saying concerning this sparrow, "They neither sow nor reap nor gather into barns; yet your heavenly Father feeds them."[70]

Truly, O my Master Lord, these sparrows are better than many men, but because of Your exceeding love and encouragement of us, we who are weak, You said something that puts us to shame, that is, "Are you not of more value than they?"[71]

We learn from them the life of faith, not caring about the material things, nor worrying about tomorrow. And You, Yourself, Lord said to us that we should look at the birds of the air and learn. Perhaps You meant that we are of more value than they, in that we are rational beings, who have a spirit, [who are created] in the image of God and according to His likeness—and even though the birds are better than us in their trusting in You!

I also liked in the sparrow the release and love of freedom. I liked that it did not shackle itself to a particular place, the source of its living, so that I said in a poem which I composed about an anchorite:

---

68   Matthew 6:34.
69   Matthew 6:25.
70   Matthew 6:26.
71   Ibid.

No monastery have I, for my monastery
is all hills and deserts.

A bird I am, roaming in the air,
having no desire for nests.

Unfettered I am in the world,
in my marching and rests.[72]

A Lesson from the Ant

We can also take a lesson on industriousness from the ant. And so does the book of Proverbs say to us, "Go to the ant, you sluggard! Consider her ways and be wise."[73] I testify with all certainty that in my whole life I have not seen an ant which is not moving. They do not stand still at all, rather they are always striving and moving. As the Scripture says that [the ant] "provides her supplies in the summer, and gathers her food in the harvest."[74] It is a marvelous lesson on industriousness and always being on the move[75].

A Lesson from the Bee

A bee is a lesson for us on orderliness. For the kingdom of the bees as Ahmad Shawky, the prince

---

72 Literally: in my dwelling and marching.

73 Proverbs 6:6; also see Proverbs 6:7–9.

74 Proverbs 6:8.

75 "Always being on the move" is literally "movement."

45

of poets, said, "is a kingdom managed, by a woman governed, and the burden of dominion is borne by the laborers and workers." Truly marvelous is the orderliness of the kingdom of the bees, whether in the distribution of the work, the production of wax in its beautiful appearance, the gathering of nectar and making honey from it, or the production of the queens' food which we steal and sell in pharmacies under the name Royal Jelly. How marvelous is the honey the bees produce, and how marvelous are its benefits to the human health, concerning which books and publications have been written. Is this not the Baptist's food?

Learning from Rites

All the rites the Church has put in place have spiritual benefits to the one who desires to meditate and learn. For this reason, we find that children and the illiterate benefit, though their educational and intellectual level may not help them in understanding the doctrines, nor even in understanding all the meanings of the prayers. Not only these, but all the congregation obtains spiritual benefits from the rites.

They benefit from all that they see of candles, incense, icons, garments. They also benefit from the movements of the priests, and from being in its midst or in the Sanctuary. They likewise spiritually benefit from the church steps, from standing up and sitting down, from the appearance of the garments and crosses, etc.

They see a candle lit in front of an icon of a saint, so they are reminded of the story of the saint and benefit by him. And they see the honor the church bestows on him through lights, so they know

47

that he must have been profitable and worthy of honor. And so God honors those who honor Him. And the candle light reminds them of how this saint was luminous like this candle. And so as to give light like a candle, he must be set apart and must melt in giving light. And they take a lesson on self-sacrifice for the sake of the love of God, and on serving others.

They feel that this saint is alive and has not died, so they speak with him and seek his prayers on their behalf. They converse with him as though he were present among them. And so they acquire an idea about the relationship between the Church striving on earth and Her members who strove and departed. And in all that—and without knowing it—the doctrine of immortality becomes rooted in them, and within themselves they repeat the saying of the priest in the prayer, "For there is no death for Your servants, but a departure."[76] All these are lessons from a mere candle and icon.

And those who have delved deeper see that the candle gives light because of the oil which is in it, and that the oil is a symbol of the Holy Spirit. Therefore, they see that all the good that we do is not ascribed to our good substance as much as it is ascribed to the work of the Spirit in us. They also remember the importance of oil in the parable of the wise and foolish virgins.

---

76   Saturday Offering of Morning Incense.

They take other lessons from candles when the Gospel is read, and from the candles in church and the sanctuary, in general. They remember the saying of the psalm, "Your word is a lamp to my feet and a light to my path,"[77] and, "The commandment of the LORD is pure, enlightening the eyes."[78] And they see that the church is as heaven in her lights, and that these lights remind us of the angels, and that the believers "shall shine ... like the stars forever and ever."[79]

The white priest garments remind those praying of the purity of the priesthood, and that the priests are angels of the church,[80] and remind them of the inhabitants of heaven who appear in the Book of Revelation with white robes which they made white in the blood of the Lamb.[81]

The steps which the priests ascend to the Sanctuary remind them of the sublimity of the Altar and of it being exalted, and of the loftiness of its servants. And so they take off their shoes before entering the Sanctuary, feeling its holiness. They are also reminded that the position of the deacons and servants is higher from that of the congregation, and that the position of the Sanctuary is higher than both.

---

77   Psalms 119:105.

78   Psalms 19:8.

79   Daniel 12:3.

80   See Revelation 2–3.

81   See Revelation 7:13–14.

And the incense, rising up, being a sweet-smelling aroma, reminds them of the pure prayers that ascend up to heaven.

Time fails me to speak of all the rites of the Church in detail, and all the meditations and lessons they contain, with the diversity of readings, hymns, and prayers—there is need of books [to speak of them].

It is sufficient that everyone entering church with the spirit of meditation, comes out in a strong spiritual state, having been affected by the lessons which he received from the rites.

The mere sight of a church reminds them of Noah's ark and how the children of God were saved in it; or it reminds them of heaven and of the angels and the light it contains.

And the [church] tower which rises up on high toward heaven reminds them, before entering church, to lift up their own eyes on high, directing them upwardly.

Whoever desires to be discipled finds rich material in the rites.

Discipleship unto Occurrences

Every occurrence that takes place harbors in its depths a profitable lesson to whoever desires to profit and to be discipled. Not only do the righteous profit, but also the people of the world.

When King Ahasuerus read the book of the records of the chronicles, his soul was moved by what he read. And this was a cause for the salvation of all the people. Occurrences inspire particular feelings and lead those who are moved by them to spiritual actions.

I wish that we contemplate God's hand in everything that happens with us and around us, to individuals and groups.

We take a lesson on God, how He acts, how and when He intervenes, how He transforms evil to good, how He manages the matters of this world in wisdom, [in a manner] combining the freedom which He grants to man with the Divine strictness which establishes justice upon the earth.

We take lessons on God's care, God's justice, and God's patience and longsuffering.

David the prophet recorded occurrences that took place in his days. David sang them in his psalms, and the people [of Judah] sang them in their songs in the Book of Jasher.[82] And they were lessons. And likewise the occurrences which Joshua sang[83] were also recorded in the book of the national songs, known as the Book of Jasher.

Contemplate then all the occurrences you pass through, and take a lesson from them, and keep them in your heart. As it was said about the Virgin, that she "kept all these things in her heart."[84] The Lord also established certain memorials of special events, that the people may not forget them; the stones, for example, which they placed in the midst of the Jordan River, that they may not forget that it was split one day.[85]

The story of the crossing of the Red Sea and the story of the three youths, the Church placed in Midnight Praises, that we may sing them every day and take a lesson on faith and on God's care and protection. And there are other stories beside these two.

Also the occurrences we read in the Synaxarion

---

82   See 2 Samuel 1:18.

83   See Joshua 10:13.

84   Luke 2:51.

85   See Joshua 4:9.

everyday are nothing but other lessons we are discipled unto. They are read to us that we may be discipled unto the occurrences, and that we may perceive how God acted and how the saints acted. Other stories from the Book of Acts we hear in the [Divine] Liturgy, for the same purpose, and yet other stories from the lives of the saints. Blessed is the one who profits from all these occurrences, [taking] lessons.

They may be called lessons from history if they took place in the past, and lessons from occurrences if they took place in our generation, and we witnessed them with our eyes or heard about them with our ears.

To let occurrences, however, pass by without taking lessons from them, this undoubtedly is negligence in discipleship. Even the people of the world find in occurrences a moral, that is, lessons a person learns from and profits by, whether they happen to him or to others, a friend or foe. The poet said:

He who keeps history in his chest
Adds years to his life.

Discipleship unto the Father of Confession

Happy is the man whose father of confession is at the level of spiritual guidance. Not only does he listen and read the absolution, but he also guides and teaches, and explains the spiritual path, and grants his child in confession the gift of discretion and discernment.

This is the teacher, who has studied the spiritual path and experienced it; has studied the human soul, has known its weaknesses, its instincts, its inclinations, its motives. He has also studied the warfare of the demons, their devices, cunning, and deception; and he has also knowledge of the ways to overcome them.

Such a father you may be discipled unto.

If such a person cannot be found, the confessant should look for a spiritual guide beside the father of confession. It is preferable that the father of confession be the guide, for the soul of the person is laid bare before him. However, if he did not possess this gift, or if his time were extremely tight, insufficient to guide the hundreds of confessants, in addition to his other responsibilities, then necessity demands that there should be [another as] a guide. [This latter] supports the confessant by his advice and encouragement, and reveals to him [the confessant] what is beyond his knowledge so that he does not walk in a daze.

With respect to discipleship unto the fathers [of confession] and guides, we have the following remarks:

1. The guide must be sound in his doctrine, sound in his guidance and direction, tested and experienced. Otherwise, the saying of the Scripture would apply, that "if the blind leads the blind, both will fall into a ditch."[86] This is the state which the Lord criticized with respect to the scribes and Pharisees, and said about them that they are "blind guides."[87] And He said to them, reprovingly, "For you travel land and sea to win one proselyte, and when he is won, you make him twice as much a son of hell as yourselves."[88]

2. Then, if the father [of confession] and guide deviates, one must not obey him, and

---

86   Matthew 15:14.

87   Matthew 23:16, 24.

88   Matthew 23:15.

his guidance must not be accepted. From this standpoint, the person ought to seek guidance, and at the same time, ought to be watchful[89]. He should ensure that his conscience is at peace with all the guidance he receives. And the father or guide should not be content with giving directions only, but also should convince and give proof of the teaching, through Scriptural verses or stories and sayings of the saints.

3. There is no objection to that a person asks their teacher or guide or spiritual father [for clarification]. For the disciples of the Lord Christ Himself used to ask Him and seek clarification on some matters. And He—glory be to His name— would explain to them, give them parables, mention verses from the Scriptures to them and interpret [them].[90] Therefore, if someone finds in their guide's advice what is contrary to the word of God, let them remember the saying of the Scripture, "We ought to obey God rather than men."[91]

4. It is not good that the confessants try to be an [exact] image of their spiritual father in everything. For perhaps what suites their father is not suitable for them. And perhaps their father's circumstances, abilities, and psychological makeup are completely different from their own. Rather, they should take the principles and apply them

---

89   Literally: open-eyed.

90   See Luke 24:27.

91   Acts 5:29.

according to the measure of their spiritual capacity, and according to what is suitable for them and what suites their personality.

5. At the same time, the guide must not abolish the personality of the person, to whom they are discipled. He must not make the disciple walk in his own current by coercion, without taking into consideration the disciple's circumstances, psychological makeup, and inclination! For example, if the guide is a lover of solitude and stillness, he must not impel all his disciples to solitude. For some of them may have a social personality, who love to serve people and be with them, and benefit them and be benefited from them.

6. It is possible for a person to have more than one guide, asking each of them on the things he has mastered, so that there may not be discrepancies between the directions. But if this thing happens or the like, the person should take it as an occasion to ask, to study, to [acquire] more information, and to counter an opinion with an opinion—without embarrassment and without mentioning names.

Abba Anthony the Great took lessons from all the ascetics around him, in the beginning of his monastic life. He learned meekness from one, silence from another, asceticism and renunciation from a third, prayer and meditation from a fourth, wisdom from a fifth, etc.

7. A person may be required to advance

gradually in what they receive from their guide or from books. For not all the virtues, of which a person is convinced, are easy to implement. Perhaps they need time, and a long time too, because of the soul's being unaccustomed to these new virtues, or perhaps because of the habit's resistance, or because of the demons' warfare and their attempt to hinder the person on the path of God, or because of the obstacles which a person encounters from their family or the surrounding environment.

Also the thing, which a person attains easily, might be lost easily, [too]. For it is not important that a person practices a particular virtue; rather, what is important is to remain steadfast in it, until it becomes second nature to them. Therefore, every virtue, in which a person does not remain [steadfast] for a time, may be transient in their life and inconstant.

For it is inappropriate for a person to make big leaps in the spiritual path and to try to arrive before the time. Rather, with calmness, deliberation, and balance, they should walk step by step, until they arrive through steady steps, and "not to think of himself more highly than he ought to think."[92] And they should not hasten to a particular degree before mastering what is before it, and should not pressure their guide and spiritual father to permit them [to pursue] with such haste.

---

92   Romans 12:3.

8. You must not consider your spiritual father a mere machine that executes the spiritual wishes you present. You should not present to him decisions that must be executed; rather, mere wishes, or more rightly, mere suggestions or questions or aspirations, concerning which he would tell you whether they are good for you or not. Do not pressure him to give you the permission to implement, and do not become angry if he does not give you the permission. Otherwise, the guidance would be a charade, and in this case you would be as though someone who is walking according to their own will. They, however, want an approval from the father [of confession] to give spiritual lawfulness to their will and wishes.

9. Before seeking spiritual guidance, you must pray that God may grant to your guide a good thought that suites your life. That is to say, you should pray that God may implement His will in your life through this father or guide. God guides him to that which he guides you with, so he directs you with the guidance which God desires to present to you.

10. Know that the virtues which you follow according to your own will may lead you to vainglory. Therefore, the fathers in *the Paradise* say that "If you see a young man ascending to heaven of his own free will, seize him by the foot and drag him down, for it is to his advantage."[93] The danger

---

93   *The Anonymous Sayings of the Desert Fathers*, J. Wortley, trans.

here in this statement is "of his own free will." Also the Scripture says, "Lean not on your own understanding."[94]

The Scripture explained this matter in a verse which was repeated twice, within close proximity in the same Book, and this is: "There is a way that seems right to a man, but its end is the way of death."[95] A person may cling to this way which appears right, yet in it—and in his clinging [to it]—there is utmost harm to him. And perhaps this way which appears right to him is of the deception of the demons. On this point specifically, Abba Isaac and St. Evagrius have copious explanations, in that the one who clings to his thought, who directs himself according to his own will, may persuade himself that this thought is from God and that the Spirit is the One who inspired this thought in him!

11. How dangerous is the state of those who say that they receive their knowledge from God directly, and that they are discipled unto Christ directly. And therefore they refuse to be discipled unto people. At the same time, they cannot be sure whether the thought, which came to them, is from God or not! What is marvelous is that those who say such words are neither prophets nor one of the twelve. Nor can they say as Paul the Apostle said, "For I received from the Lord that which I also

---

(Cambridge, UK: Cambridge University Press, 2013), N111.

94   Proverbs 3:5.

95   Proverbs 14:12 and 16:25.

delivered to you."[96]

12. Being taught by God may mean learning from the Divine sources. We are taught by God through His Holy Scriptures. We are taught by the Lord Christ through His holy life. Nevertheless, there is a need for someone to interpret these Books to us, and for someone to lead us in the spiritual path. For learning is not so much the mere theoretical understanding, as it is the practical application.

13. Otherwise, why did God create [or establish] teachers and guides? Why did He say to His disciples, "[Go], teaching them to observe all things that I have commanded you,"[97] if it were possible for a person to be taught by God directly? And why was it said, "He Himself gave some to be ... pastors and teachers"?[98] And why was it said, "He who teaches, in teaching"?[99] Also why was it said that from the mouth of the priest the law is sought?[100]

As for the statement, "And they shall all be taught by God,"[101] we understand it through another verse, which is, "He who hears you hears Me."[102]

The one who seeks to be taught by God directly,

---

96   1 Corinthians 11:23.

97   Matthew 28:20.

98   Ephesians 4:11.

99   Romans 12:7.

100 See Malachi 2:7.

101 John 6:45.

102 Luke 10:16.

or to be discipled unto Christ directly, perhaps lacks the humility which accepts teaching from teachers and guides, and is in need of remembering the saying of the Apostle, "Remember those who rule over you[103], who have spoken the word of God to you,"[104] and, "Obey those who rule over you, and be submissive, for they watch out for your souls, as those who must give account. Let them do so with joy and not with grief, for that would be unprofitable for you."[105]

St. Paul the Apostle praised his disciple Timothy the Bishop, saying, "You have carefully followed my doctrine, manner of life, purpose, faith."[106] Why did he not advise him that his doctrine and manner of life were from God directly? Are we, I wonder, greater than St. Timothy who received his teaching from Paul the Apostle? And why does St. Paul say to the believers, "Imitate me, just as I also imitate Christ,"[107] and, "Brethren, join in following my example"[108]?

14. The thought that rejects discipleship unto the Church, and wants to be taught by God directly, is neither an Orthodox, nor is it a Biblical, Scriptural thought. This is in light of the verses of

---

103 Arabic verse may be translated to, "Remember your guides."
104 Hebrews 13:7.
105 Ibid.
106 2 Timothy 3:10.
107 1 Corinthians 11:1.
108 Philippians 3:17.

the Scriptures we [previously] mentioned, and many more like them, of which are verses talking about teaching, evangelism, guidance, preaching, and the church's function in teaching. In all the churches of the world—no matter how different their doctrines are—there are preachers and pulpits for preaching. What would be the point of all these if people were to be taught by God directly?

15. The spiritual life, brethren, requires humility of heart. And [there is] humility in discipleship. The one, however, who insists on being taught by God directly, may fall into pride. And pride, [in turn], can hand him over a prey to the demons, so they present to him what they like of teaching. All innovators and heretics, in the history of the Church, refused to be discipled unto the Church, and followed their thought, thinking that this thought was from God.

16. How do you truly know that the thought, which you think is from God, is truly from God? It is related in the *Paradise* [*of the Holy Fathers*] concerning Abba Macarius the Great that a thought came to him, [urging him] to visit the anchorites [dwelling] in the inner desert, so this great saint says, "I remained three years wrestling with this thought, to see whether it was from God or not."[109] Yet you simply see that you are taught by God directly, and

---

109 Cf. *Give Me a Word: The Alphabetical Sayings of the Desert Fathers*, J. Wortley, trans. (Yonkers, NY: SVS Press, 2014), Macarius the Egyptian 2.

that the spirit says to you, "so and so"!

Which spirit is this? And how can you be sure? The Scripture says, "Do not believe every spirit, but test the spirits, whether they are of God; because many false prophets have gone out into the world."[110] It also says, "Test all things."[111]

17. There are perhaps many sources of the thought which you think is from God. It may be your own thought or your own inclination. It may be a thought settled in your subconscious from things you previously read and heard. And it may be a deception of the devil. You need to tarry and deliberate, to read the Scriptures, and to ask and seek guidance.

Beloved, be humble and become disciples, and "remember those who rule over you, who have spoken the word of God to you."[112]

---

110 1 John 4:1.

111 1 Thessalonians 5:21.

112 Hebrews 13:7.

www.ingramcontent.com/pod-product-compliance
Lightning Source LLC
Chambersburg PA
CBHW020951030426
42339CB00004B/54